the

SPEAKER'S
Quick
Guide

TO TECHNICAL
PRESENTATIONS

Overcome the Nine Major Pitfalls
Between You and Getting Your Point Across

DAVID P. OTEY

Published by Speaking of Solutions, LLC, P.O. Box 1322, Golden, CO 80402

ISBN: 978-0-9992744-2-2

Dedicated to Jerry Otey Correu—my first reading teacher, my first audience, and the first reader of all my books.

CONTENTS

PREFACE

The second book in the *Speaker's Quick Guide* series is intended, like its predecessor, to be a concise, practical resource for speakers seeking to improve their skills. Unlike the first book, however, this one is written specifically for the scientist, engineer, or other technical professional charged with presenting a technical topic. That's not to say other readers won't benefit, only that the technical presenter and his or her particular challenges are the focus.

With thousands of books available on the topic of technical presentations, why add one more to the mix? I can think of a couple of reasons. First, consider the time pressure you may be under if you have been tapped with giving a presentation. This book, as its name implies, is designed to help you quickly. You can probably read it in under two hours. Because its rich content is distilled from what I have learned through years of public speaking, coaching, and studying how we communicate and process information, this book has no fluff. You will quickly find insights into the mistakes you might make—because you have seen other presenters make them—and you will also find a road map for avoiding those pitfalls as you prepare your presentation.

Second, I have been where you are. With a degree in physics and a 25-year career in engineering, I understand your analytical mind and the challenges you face in communicating about your work to a variety of audiences, be they technical or laypersons. You expect content that is directly applicable to your situation, with a sound basis for any claims it makes, and with depth. That is what you will find here.

So let us consider what this book is and what it is not. It is a concise compilation of tools and practices that, if used and followed with intelligence and commitment, will make you a better presenter. It combines research, personal experience, and much of what I have learned from world-class speakers and coaches as I have made the transition from engineer to professional speaker. It is a road map to that elusive goal of connecting with your audience so that your information will make a difference to them.

This is not a book on how to make your presentations prettier by animating your slides or using fancier display technology, or how to be a more entertaining presenter. The tips and tools you will find in this book will not lead you to do anything that will cause people to take you and your work any less seriously, because I know that is important to you.

So, congratulations. You have been given the task of making a presentation about your work. Let's get started.

The first thing you need to know is that you have an obligation to your audience not to bore them. Boredom is actually a bigger problem than you might think, as you will discover in Chapter 1. The next three chapters will lay out, in three logical groupings, the most common pitfalls I see technical presenters fall into. Based on what you discover in those three chapters, you will then be ready for Chapter 5, "The Way Out of the Pit." In it you will find a detailed process that, if followed, will lead you away from those nine pitfalls.

No matter how well you prepare your talk, however, you are likely to encounter that completely unscripted portion, the dreaded question-and-answer (Q&A) session. Handling that with grace and professionalism will be the topic of Chapter 6. I will then close by describing the results you can expect to achieve by using the guidance you find on these pages.

By the time you are done with this book, I am confident that you will be equipped to give a more engaging, successful presentation, and that you will share in that confidence.

CHAPTER 1

Identifying the Problem

"There are no boring subjects, only disinterested minds."

G.K. CHESTERTON

You can be glad you weren't there to witness my first foray into the world of public speaking. It was in the early 1990s, and the occasion was a national conference of the Society of Broadcast Engineers (SBE). I had submitted a paper, and the Society had chosen it to be among those presented at the conference. Recently promoted to the position of chief engineer at an Austin, Texas, TV station, I thought rather highly of myself. And when SBE selected my paper for the annual conference, my head got even bigger.

Then I went to Houston to present my paper. Picture an oversized room at a large convention center. A huge projection screen. The lights are dim. Chairs are mostly empty. It is a mid-afternoon session. Fortunately, there was a microphone on the lectern. Without it, I'm not sure I could have drowned out the snoring.

I didn't know how to present a paper. I didn't know the first thing about connecting with an audience. Didn't know anything about finding a story in my information. Didn't understand that I was there to fulfill a need for that audience. It was all about my need to show off what I knew. And what did I do for that audience?

I committed the unpardonable sin. I bored them.

Let us consider that claim for a moment. Is boredom a serious problem for presenters? Or is it merely a byproduct of the fact that some audience members will be more engaged with the topic than others? And if it is a problem, is it the presenter's problem or the audience members'?

I contend that your audience's boredom is not simply a byproduct or a symptom. Rather, it is a serious problem—and it is your problem, because boredom blocks effective information transfer. In other words, it undermines your very purpose in giving a presentation.

Why is boredom the real problem?

Science knows surprisingly little about boredom, but what is known supports this point. According to the website LiveScience.com:

> *A 2012 review of boredom research that was conducted in educational settings suggested*

> *that boredom is some combination of an objective lack of neurological excitement and a subjective psychological state of dissatisfaction, frustration or disinterest, all of which result from a lack of stimulation.*[1]

In short, if you are boring your audience, not only are they dissatisfied with your presentation, but also you are failing to stimulate their brains. Is that what you want? Of course not!

Some will contend that boredom is a delivery problem. That it results from a monotonous vocal pattern or a lack of energy on the part of the presenter. Some claim that the cure for boredom is a different, perhaps less static, method of presenting visuals. Or even that inserting music, movement, or unrelated images into a presentation will sufficiently relieve the audience's boredom and re-engage them in the message.

I disagree.

I hold with those who say that boredom is not a delivery problem; it is a content problem. What does that mean? It means that to be a successful presenter, you must understand what contributes to boredom and learn to eliminate it from the very beginning of your preparation process, if your goal of information transfer is going to have any chance of success.

If boredom is the problem, what is the solution?

For several years, I have been drawing upon what I have learned about public speaking to coach other speakers.

[1] https://www.livescience.com/56162-science-of-boredom.html, accessed 5 July 2019

When I tell technical presenters that they have an obligation not to bore their audience, what I often hear in response is, "But I'm here to deliver information, not to entertain!" I didn't say you have to be entertaining. But the opposite of boredom is not entertainment. It is engagement.

When your audience members are engaged, they will be interested in what you have to say. They will be curious. They will want to know more. Engagement, not information delivery, must be your goal when you speak. Create engagement, and successful information transfer will follow.

How do you create engagement? That is truly what this whole book is about. Here is a sneak preview of the key: empathy.

Empathy can be defined as the ability to understand and share the feelings of another. It is an emotional connection. What place does emotion have in an information-rich presentation? In the absence of an emotional connection, your information simply goes nowhere. For your information to make a difference to your listeners, they must make three decisions:

1. To *accept* your information.
2. To *remember* your information.
3. To *act* on your information.

To do so, they must access their decision-making center, which is located in the emotional part of the brain. No emotional connection with you means those decisions will not go in your favor.

But when you create empathy in the minds of your

listeners, they will want your solution to their problem. They will see you as someone they can relate to, who understands their condition and has information that will improve their condition. Every step you take in preparing your presentation should be taken with this in mind.

Fortunately, there is a scientifically proven technique you can employ to create empathy, and that is to tell the story of your work.

What does that mean, exactly?

You may have heard of oxytocin, the neurotransmitter that facilitates empathy. It is sometimes called the "bonding hormone." It turns out that one of the things that triggers oxytocin production is hearing a story. Especially a story with a character you can relate to, who strives for something that is initially unattainable because of some obstacle. When we in the audience experience how that character overcomes the obstacle and is changed in the process, we will want what that character wants. By triggering our oxytocin, the storyteller elicits our empathy. You will learn more about this in Chapter 3.

In sum, boredom *is* your problem. And it is a content problem, not a delivery or display technology problem. To prevent boredom, you must create engagement with your audience. The following chapters detail nine mistakes technical presenters typically make that get in the way of engagement and allow boredom to flourish. Once you understand what these mistakes are and why they are mistakes (even though you may have seen many presenters make them), then you will be ready to learn a content-creation process that facilitates connection and engagement.

CHAPTER 2

Pitfalls, Part 1: Organization and Planning

"Plans are worthless, but planning is everything."

DWIGHT D. EISENHOWER

As you saw in Chapter 1, your most important task as a presenter is to create audience engagement so information transfer will follow. But most presenters think their most important task is to deliver information. This false belief leads them to commit a series of mistakes, the net result of which is disconnection and boredom. In this and the following two chapters, you will see nine of those common mistakes, or pitfalls, laid bare. Please note that I, too, made these mistakes when I was first starting out as a speaker. Here are the first four pitfalls, which I group under the heading "Organization and Planning." For each pitfall, you will also see what to do to avoid it in your own presentation.

1. No specific purpose

The first mistake is to start preparing your presentation with no clear purpose in mind. I am not referring to the *general* purpose, which can be stated in two words, such as "to inform" or "to educate" or perhaps "to persuade." A general purpose is fine, but the mistake most presenters make is not going deeper to find their *specific* purpose.

Your specific purpose is the answer to this question: *What do I want my listeners to think, do, or feel differently when I am done?* In other words, what difference do you want to make? How are you going to change the condition of your listeners? If you're not there to make a difference, then you really ought not give a presentation. You should just hand people printed information. But you are giving a presentation because, instinctively, you know that people engage with a speaker in a different way than they engage with the printed word.

So think carefully about your specific purpose. What do you want your listeners to think, do, or feel differently when you are done? It may be a combination of two or even all three of those things. In a scientific presentation, for example, you might want fellow scientists to *think* differently about the question at the heart of your research. Or you may want people to *act*, such as deciding to accept your engineering solution, to fund further research, or even to collaborate with you. And there is a place even in a technical presentation for the third element: *feeling.* What do you want your audience to *feel* differently? Perhaps you're speaking to people who have provided funding for your research. You want them to feel confident that it was money well spent.

What do you want your listeners to think, do, or feel differently when you are done? Once you know the answer to that question, that becomes the filter through which every piece of content—every sentence, every paragraph, every image—must pass before it is allowed into your presentation. If it does not support your specific purpose, it does not go in.

2. No thought given to the audience's needs

A successful presentation starts not with your need to present, but with *an understanding of what your audience needs from you.* If you want to connect successfully with your listeners and get your point across, you must start with an understanding of your audience members and their needs. Every member of your audience is silently asking himself or herself this question: "What's in it for me?" All too often, speakers make the mistake of ignoring this question.

I know this is a serious mistake because I've made it. When I started working on the training project that eventually led me out of broadcast engineering and into my current career as a speaker and coach, I, along with the other engineers on the project, made the classic engineer's mistake: We thought the training had to be all about the technology. Explain the new technology clearly enough, and everything will be fine, we thought.

We tried that, and the initial trials were not well received. So I took another approach. I spent time with some of the technicians who were the target audience for this training. They didn't express curiosity about the technology. They expressed fear that it was going to make their job skills obsolete. I had one tell me, "I'm afraid of getting yelled at—or worse, fired!"

So, we went back and created a new curriculum that was much less technology-heavy. Instead, we showed them how little their job would actually change as a result of rolling out this new technology, and how those changes they did encounter would actually make their job easier and give them more confidence that they were doing it well. In fact, our training goal—although we never said this to them in so many words—was not to increase their information so much as it was to reduce their fear and anxiety. That project was a complete success. In 33 months, we trained more than 10,000 people in 900 locations, and not a single person came back and said, "We can't use the new technology due to inadequate training."

It was successful because we came to understand our audience's needs. You now know about the specific purpose: what you want your listeners to think, do, or feel differently when you are done. To achieve that requires that you know something about your audience and their needs. How do you find out? Ask them. Do your research. Or, at the very least, put yourself in their shoes and ask, "What need would drive me to be in this audience, waiting to hear this speaker? What would I be wanting to get out of this presentation?"

3. Starting out with your visuals

In addition to starting their preparation with no specific purpose, many—dare I say *most?*—technical presenters make the mistake of beginning their preparation by creating their visuals. They seem to think that the way to start preparing for a presentation is to begin assembling a PowerPoint® deck. (I know we made this mistake early on in the process of creating the training program I described earlier. We had to learn the hard way!) Once the slides are created and placed in order, all you have to do is look at them and narrate them, right?

Wrong! That is the surefire way to alienate your audience instead of connecting with them. Remember from Chapter 1: You must *create engagement first*, and then information transfer will follow. In other words, put *connection* before *content*.

If you begin your process by focusing on how you are going to illustrate your talk instead of what you are going to say to meet your audience's needs and fulfill your specific purpose, then you are "putting the cart before the horse," to use an old expression. Once you start down that road, you will have a hard time being audience-focused and making the kind of connection that ensures your ideas take root and flourish.

Though you may not realize it, you have almost certainly seen presenters make this mistake. How do you know they have made it? Here are the telltale signs:

1. Their attention tends to be on their slides, not on the audience.

2. If something goes wrong, like a slide out of order or a projection problem, they get flustered because they are using their slides as a crutch; they can't present without them.
3. The audience is bored!

4. Lack of preparation

Closely related to the error of beginning the preparation with the visuals is the error of not preparing at all. Perhaps you already have slides and you think that concludes your preparation process. Maybe you have already written a paper about your work, so you think all you must do is lift some illustrations and key bullet points, put them on the screen in the right order, and you're done. (This describes exactly how I let my audience down in Houston, in that story I told in Chapter 1.)

The telltale signs a presenter has made this mistake are essentially the same as in the previous section. In most cases, the presenter will be too attentive to the slides to know what to say next, and inattentive to the audience and their needs.

Consider what is at stake when you give a presentation. Are you looking for widespread acceptance of your research finding or your solution to an engineering problem? Are you looking for collaborators? Are you seeking funding to continue your work? Perhaps it is a sales presentation and you are making the case that your firm is the one best equipped to solve that prospective customer's problem. Or perhaps your next job or promotion depends on how well this presentation goes. When you consider all that might be at stake, does it make any sense to go into that presentation less than extremely well prepared?

In Chapter 5, you will discover a step-by-step preparation process. If you follow it, you will begin with an understanding of your audience's needs and your specific purpose in delivering your information to that audience. You will learn how to create and refine what you want to say and how you want to connect with that audience before you ever create your first slide.

Overall, this chapter has shown you how common pitfalls in the preparation stage will doom you to disconnection. Before you can benefit from the process in Chapter 5, however, you must also learn to recognize the common pitfalls in content and structure, which will be the subject of Chapter 3.

CHAPTER 3

Pitfalls, Part 2: Content and Structure

"Everything starts with a structure."

PATRICIA FRIPP, HALL OF FAME SPEAKER

Chapter 2 covered the pitfalls speakers commonly fall into in the preparation stage (or lack thereof) of creating a presentation. In this chapter, you will see the two major pitfalls that occur within the content of the presentation itself. Even if your intentions are good with respect to knowing your specific purpose and what your audience needs from you, and even if you prepare correctly (instead of starting with the visuals), you will still lose your audience if you commit these two errors. The first is a lack of structure, and the second is lack of a story.

5. Lack of structure

Imagine this: You are sitting in an auditorium listening to a speaker. The speaker has interesting information and effective delivery techniques. You feel engaged and attentive. Afterward, a friend who was not present asks you to restate the main points of the presentation.

You can't recall them.

What you witnessed was likely a speech with no structure.

And have you ever given a speech where you had to keep looking at the slides to remember what you wanted to say next? What you actually gave was likely a speech with no structure, and that's why you had a hard time remembering it.

Lack of structure makes it hard for both the presenter and the audience to remember anything. That is why so much advice on speaking relates to structure. Whether it's the three-point outline or the venerable "Tell them what you're going to tell them; tell them; and tell them what you told them," you have no doubt heard advice on how to give a speech structure.

And yet, so many speakers fail to do this. I have even failed to do this! Remember the training program I described in Chapter 2, the one where we engineers thought the problem we were trying to solve was lack of information about the new technology? You will recall that the initial trials of the curriculum we created were not well received. One reason was that we (like so many engineers before us) were guilty of performing what is colloquially known as a "data dump." We had collected so much information on the new technology—

and illustrated it with spiffy, animated slides—that we believed we wouldn't be done until we had dumped all that information on our unsuspecting audiences.

Thus, when we started over, we started with a structure. The structure of the hundreds of training sessions was always the same:

1. Show a video illustrating how people like them were currently performing their job with the legacy technology.
2. Show another video illustrating how other people were doing the same job but using the new technology.
3. Lead a discussion of the observed differences between the two.
4. Use demo equipment to create scenarios like the ones they were likely to encounter.
5. Take questions, using the demo equipment to answer them where possible.

In this way, even though the trainees and the demo equipment may have been thousands of miles apart (it was distance learning using satellite-delivered video), our trainees came away satisfied that they would be able to use their own new equipment successfully once it was in place. The trainees remembered what they had observed and discovered, and our trainers never got lost in the middle.

This is just one example of how to structure your talk. There are many ways to do so. Perhaps the most common is a chronological structure, in which your points unfold as events on a timeline. Or there may be another logical way to flow from one point to another. The key is to have a structure, and not to simply start talking and hope you find a way to bring your train of thought into the station.

Closely related to giving your speech structure is to create a road map that makes your purpose clear to your audience from the beginning. In the Preface of this book, for example, I gave you such a road map. I briefly described the organization plan of the book. And at key transition points, I have reminded you of what you have already encountered and what is coming up. You can do the same thing when you speak.

The key is to do that while engaging the audience with "you" language. Instead of "Today, I want to tell you about..." (because really, do your listeners care what you want?), practice giving your road map this way:

> *Today, you are going to pick up three tools for giving more effective presentations. First, you will discover the power of the specific purpose statement. Second, you will see the power of using "you" language to draw your listeners in. And finally, you will pick up a storytelling model that will ensure a higher level of emotional connection with your audience.*

In this way, you make the structure clear to all, from the beginning. And not just the structure but also the benefits the listener stands to gain from hearing you speak.

On the other hand, if you fail to make your structure clear, you will miss the opportunity to take hold of your listeners' curiosity and lead them by the hand through your content. And when they get lost, the predictable result will be confusion or boredom, or both. This pitfall can cost you dearly!

6. Lack of story

Along with structure, there is another (often missing) ingredient necessary for making your message memorable, and that is a story. Yes, even the most technical of presentations needs a story. Many presenters seem unaware of the importance of telling the story of their work. Yet, every successful public speaker knows the maxim "Tell a story; make a point." For your audience to make the conscious decision to *accept*, *remember*, and *act on* your information, you must first make a connection with that audience. And the fundamental unit of human connection is the story. Not information. Not data. Certainly not charts and graphs. A story.

By "story," I do not mean a random, amusing anecdote told to get a laugh and break the monotony. I am referring to something integral to your struggle to add to the world's knowledge of your topic. Remember, you don't have to be entertaining, but you do have an obligation not to be boring. As said in Chapter 1, the opposite of boredom is not entertainment but engagement. And your best tool for engaging your audience is to share your story.

There is a sound scientific basis for this claim. I previously mentioned the neurotransmitter oxytocin (not to be confused with Oxycontin™, the highly addictive opioid). Harvard researcher Paul Zak has studied oxytocin. One of his findings is that character-driven stories cause oxytocin levels to rise. He also discovered that it is important for a story to depict a conflict or a struggle. It has to do with getting and keeping the listener's attention:

> We discovered that...a story must first sustain attention—a scarce resource in the brain—by developing tension during the narrative. ...
> My experiments show that character-driven stories with emotional content result in a better understanding of the key points a speaker wishes to make and enable better recall of these points weeks later.[2]

In short, if you want to make a connection, make a difference to your listeners, and be remembered afterward, the tool for doing that—according to experimental evidence—is a well-told story. That means a story with clearly drawn characters and a central conflict or tension. When your audience can identify with the central character's struggle—that is, what he or she is striving for and what obstacle initially prevents the attainment of it—then they will want what that central character wants. And when they see how that character is changed in the process of overcoming that obstacle, they will want that change. That is how you get your audience on your side, desiring your solution to their problem.

[2] Harvard Business Review, found at https://hbr.org/2014/10/why-your-brain-loves-good-storytelling, accessed 7/13/19

Perhaps you are wondering, "But what place does a story have in a scientific presentation?" My reply to that question is another question: Do you want your message to be remembered?

Further, what is science if not the ongoing effort to unlock the mysteries of the universe? And mysteries make great stories! The problem with most technical presentations is that the presenter wants to share his or her result only, and not the struggle to get to that result. When was the last time you saw a technical presentation that started with, "Let me tell you about all the things we tried that didn't work before we were successful"?

But you don't have to tell of *all* your failed attempts to get the oxytocin flowing. Remember what Paul Zak said: You want some tension, and then the resolution. In Volume One of this series, *The Speaker's Quick Guide to Telling Better Stories*, I describe three models for structuring a story. The simplest is the "A-B-C Model," and it works like this: *"A" wants "B" despite "C"*. That is, there is a protagonist ("A") who wants to attain or achieve something ("B") and is initially prevented from achieving that goal because of some obstacle ("C"). When you start to talk about your work using this model, you are setting up precisely what Paul Zak is talking about: a character and a tension. That character wants something that is hard to get, and the audience will want to know how he or she finally gets it.

For example, a Ph.D. student I once coached was preparing a presentation on her research into the use of nanoparticles to deliver cancer drugs. In her early drafts, she launched into what nanoparticles were, how they solved the solubility problem for cancer drugs, and what size particles were optimal for absorption by tumors. Rather dry stuff, even for her audience of pharmaceutical scientists.

After coaching, she took a different approach. "Look around the room," she said. "Approximately forty of you will be diagnosed with cancer in your lifetime. Five of you will die from it. I want to improve your odds of survival. But here is what we are up against: It's hard to convince cancer cells to absorb the drugs that will kill them. Now, what if we had a way to overcome the barriers that cancer cells put up? That's what we've been asking ourselves, and now we've found what we believe is a new way to do that."

Do see the A-B-C model at work there? Do you think that audience is more likely to *want* to know what her lab's proposed solution is? All it takes is a bit of tension from a story to engage your listeners' attention and curiosity.

Some of my coaching clients say, "But, David, what if I don't have a story to tell? I've got compelling information, and I believe I can be persuasive without telling a story!"

This is what I tell them: The fact is, you *do* have a story. It is the story of how you became convinced that the information you have is important enough to share. The story is already there; it just needs to be uncovered. Think of the following set of questions as a tool you can use to uncover the story behind your data:

- What need drove you to discover this information?
- What did this information mean to you

when you first learned it?
- What makes it so compelling it must be shared?

For a longer list of such questions, refer to Chapter 1 of *The Speaker's Quick Guide to Telling Better Stories*. Also in that book, you will find two more story models that will take you further into creating and relieving tension than the A-B-C Model alone.

Finally, when it comes to combining science (or engineering, or whatever your discipline is) with story, let me leave you with this thought. In 1609, a man named Galileo pointed a new invention—a spyglass—at the night sky. The world has never been the same since. In 1623, that same Galileo published the book *Il Saggiatore (The Assayer)*. It is considered to hold the origins of what we now call the scientific method. The book was a refutation of a book by another astronomer, Orazio Grassi, who differed with Galileo on the nature of comets. To clinch his argument, Galileo weaves a story about a man trying to understand the sound a cicada makes. And how do you think that story begins? "Once upon a time, in a very lonely place, there lived a man..."

If no less a scientific star than Galileo could appreciate the power of story to engage the imagination and convey great truths in an understandable way, then who are we to say otherwise? So, yes, deliver your information. And don't forget the oxytocin as well! *Tell your story*. That is how your information will engage and change your audience—and possibly the world.

Now you know how to make your content more memorable through structure and story. Before we move on to a process for building these into your presentation, we must consider three more common pitfalls.

CHAPTER 4

Pitfalls, Part 3: Visual Aids

"If your words or images are not on point, making them dance
in color won't make them relevant."

EDWARD TUFTE, PROFESSOR EMERITUS, YALE UNIVERSITY

Chapters 2 and 3 introduced you to six of the most common pitfalls that trip up technical presenters. In this chapter, you will encounter the final three pitfalls, all having to do with your visual aids.

For most presenters, the phrase "visual aids" equates to a PowerPoint® file projected onto a large screen. However, there are other methodologies for displaying visual aids. To be inclusive (and to avoid overuse of a trade name), I will refer to such methodologies collectively as *slideware*.

7. Confusing the visuals with the presentation

There are a lot of mistakes one can make with the visuals themselves, and we will get to some of those shortly. But the first principle to understand is that your visual aid, regardless of the technology, is only a visual aid. It is not the presentation. You are.

Unfortunately, this error is promulgated all the time by meeting planners. They'll tell their speakers, "Submit your presentation by uploading it to this website so our attendees can download it." To which I reply, "If you want me to upload my *visual aids*, I'll be happy to, but they will include a disclaimer that my slides do not make a stand-alone presentation. If people want to experience my presentation, they will have to attend it live."

(As I write this, the planners of my most current speaking engagement have just requested me to upload my visuals twice: the version I will use, and another version—if I so desire—for audience download. So they are catching on!)

What does it mean to say that "your visual aid is not your presentation—you are"? First, it means you are not there simply to narrate your slides. You are there to connect with your audience in a way that is possible only through the spoken word.

Second, it means we need to define what a presentation is, now that we know what it is not. Here is my definition: *Your presentation is everything your audience perceives you to do, to say, or to show them from the time you have their attention until the time you relinquish it.*

That means that once you are on the stage or in the front of the room, if you start by fumbling around with your technology—be it your projector or your microphone—then that is part of your presentation. It influences how your audience perceives you. And you have only a few seconds to make a good impression and get your audience on your side. You can't afford to waste those precious seconds waiting for your projector to warm up or testing your microphone. And you certainly won't form a positive impression if you are in the dark and the brightest object in the room is your projection screen, as is so often the case.

So turn the lights up. If you don't want anything on the screen until you start, have the projector on and display a black slide. Do a sound check ahead of time.

And most important, be well prepared. Be able to give your presentation without any visual aids, because sooner or later your technology will fail you. Not only that, but if you are dependent on your slides, you will never connect with your audience. And as we know, connection is essential for knowledge transfer to take place. Remember, the opposite of boredom is not entertainment—it is engagement. And few things are less engaging than a speaker who keeps looking at his or her slides to know what to say next.

Confusing the visual aids with the presentation is a common mistake, one that seems deeply rooted in the way we talk about presentations. If you want to set yourself apart and make a powerful impression on your audience, stop making this mistake. Turn the lights up, be well prepared, and embrace the fact that you are the presentation as well as the presenter.

8. Excessively dense visuals

Let me start with an acknowledgment. Much of what I have to say on the topic of visuals comes from the work of Dr. Edward Tufte, Professor Emeritus at Yale University and a highly regarded expert on the display of information. I had the pleasure of attending one of his all-day workshops some years ago. As I write this, I notice that he is preparing to go out on another workshop tour. If there's any way you can attend one, I highly recommend it.[3]

Here's what I learned from Professor Tufte: Generally, presenters use slideware badly. One reason for that is that they don't understand its limitations, which are both spatial and temporal in nature. In other words...

1. Screen resolution is much lower than print resolution. Simply put, the amount of information you can successfully display on a printed page will become a muddied mess when you try to translate it to the screen.
2. The presenter, not the viewer, decides how long the viewer is able to examine a slide, and side-by-side comparisons are often sacrificed for next-in-time comparisons, across a time dimension over which the viewer has no control.

[3] Details and schedule at https://www.edwardtufte.com/tufte/

In short, your audience members will have a hard time evaluating your visual evidence when they can neither see it clearly nor examine it at their leisure.

This is especially true of those mainstays of technical presentations: tables, charts, and graphs. (We'll address textual slides in the next section.)

If you have prepared any information graphics for a published paper, do not make the mistake of assuming that all you have to do is copy and paste them from your print document into a slideware file. Instead, you must consider the legibility of every item in the graphic—every axis label, data point, table entry, and callout—given the screen size and viewing distance that your audience members will experience. This is not an easy task. When it is done correctly, however, the resulting images will be easier to interpret from the audience members' seats.

Some presenters take the mistaken view that this process represents a "dumbing down" of their data. Not true! It represents the all-important step of considering your presentation from the audience members' perspective. To do otherwise is to show disdain for your audience and their needs—hardly a recipe for winning them to your point of view.

In the simplest case, preparing your information graphics for a live audience is a matter of reducing the information contained in one slide. Here are some examples, taken from a presentation by a student I coached a few years ago.

In version 1, the student attempts to put both the tabular and the graphical form of the data in one slide:

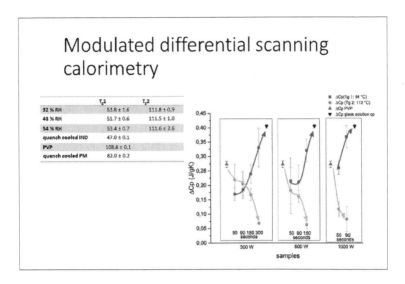

Seeing that this made the information hard to perceive visually, the student then turned to animation. First, she showed a slide with the tabular data, highlighting certain entries:

Glass solution formation

	T_g1	T_g2
32 % RH	53.8 ± 1.6	111.8 ± 0.9
43 % RH	51.7 ± 0.6	111.5 ± 1.0
54 % RH	53.4 ± 0.7	111.6 ± 2.6
quench cooled IND	47.0 ± 0.1	
PVP	108.8 ± 0.1	
quench cooled PM	82.0 ± 0.2	

Then she animated the graph to appear over the table, thus:

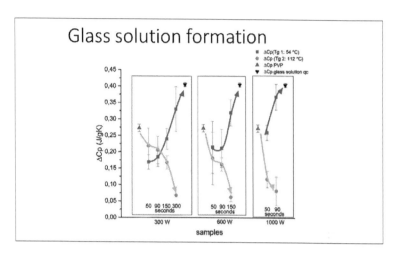

Still, though the graph is now larger, certain elements are hard to read from a distance, especially the legend at top right. What I would likely do next is to enlarge the entire image to minimize unused space, and enlarge the legend and some of the labels, as shown here:

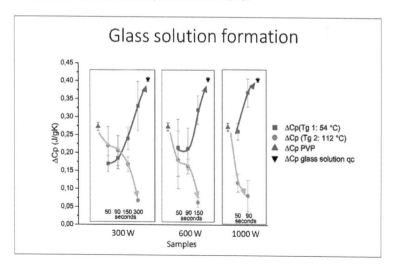

But despite these improvements to an individual slide, the presenter is still faced with the problem that the viewer has no control over how long he or she may spend examining the information graphic. Therefore, a better choice is to provide the audience with a handout containing that graphic, which audience members may then examine as they choose to. Professor Tufte points out that a single 8.5-by-11 sheet of paper (or A4, for Europeans) is capable of providing many times the information density of a computer screen or projected slide. Furthermore, if one were to take a sheet exactly twice that size (11 x 17, or A3), print on both sides and fold it in half, one effectively has a four-page handout—enough to contain quite a bit more information than the average slide deck. Those sheet sizes are readily accommodated by commercial printer/copiers. I have used this technique on any number of occasions, at only modest cost.

Of course, such a handout need not contain only figures. It can display quite a bit of text as well. That brings us to the next pitfall, relying on text slides to convey complex ideas.

9. Over-reliance on textual slides

Of all the errors one can make in using slideware, this is perhaps the most pervasive. I say this as if it is one error; actually, it is multiple errors rolled into one.

The first error arises from following some of the bad advice that is often given in the form of formulas like the "six-by-six" rule: no more than six lines of text, and no more than six words per line. Let's think about this rigorously. The average speaker of North American English speaks between 125 and

150 words per minute. The average adult reading speed is usually described as being about twice that. That means that those 36 words represent about 15 seconds of the speaker's speaking time, or about 7.5 seconds of reading time on the part of the viewer. What depth of thought is actually likely to be conveyed in that time?

Further aggravating this paucity of content is the practice of conveying information in the form of "bullet points," which are sometimes nested in an attempt to show a hierarchical relationship between statements. All too often, this has the effect of rendering complex relationships in a simplistic way. Professor Tufte calls this style "faux-analytical." [4] He has quite a bit more to say about it in the work cited below; I commend it to your reading.

The opposite problem is also a common error: creating textual slides that are too dense to be read easily on the screen. Readability is a huge problem in projected text, and one that is not easily overcome due to the number of variables involved. These include (besides the obvious font size) the projected image size, the viewing distance, projector brightness and sharpness, and ambient lighting conditions. Except for font size, these variables are likely to be unknown and uncontrollable by the person preparing the slides, so how can they possibly be optimized? "Use no less than 36-point type" is another commonly cited rule that is therefore ludicrous when examined rigorously.

---

[4] Tufte, Edward R., The Cognitive Style of PowerPoint (Cheshire, CT: Graphics Press LLC, 2003), p. 5

It might seem there is no good way to use text in projected slides, since the "sweet spot" between too little and too much is such an unknown. And in fact, keeping text slides to a minimum is one of Professor Tufte's recommendations that I wholeheartedly endorse. But even if there were a way to put the "just right" amount of text on the screen at one time, there is still a reason this is an undesirable practice. It has to do with the way the brain processes language.

Your brain has two structures involved in using language: the expressive language center and the receptive language center. The former encodes ideas into thought, and the latter—of course—does the opposite. The receptive language center is flexible in its inputs. It can take in text that you see, words that you hear spoken by others, and even words you are thinking of only in your expressive language center. But here is the key point: *It cannot take in more than one source of input at a time!*

That means that when you put words on the screen—and you are talking—you are competing with your screen for your audience members' attention. And most likely, you are losing! This is due to the simple reason that most people's attention will favor what they see over what they hear. Far better is to keep text slides to a minimum and use images (which are processed through entirely different neural pathways) that will reinforce your ideas and help make them memorable.

When images aren't appropriate, either, here is a radical idea: *Show nothing at all.* Just because there is a screen on the stage does not mean you are obligated to fill it at all times. The well-prepared presenter's best friend, when it comes to slideware, is the *black slide*. Use it whenever you want the audience's full attention to be on you. (Just be sure to tip off your audio/video support person ahead of time, as I had one approach the projector in a panic, convinced it had died.)

Ultimately, the solution to the text dilemma is the same as the solution to the previous pitfall: the judicious use of well-constructed handouts. And here I do not mean the ones that can be generated automatically by your slideware program. I mean a combination of text and information graphics that has been well laid out by someone skilled in the use of page layout software. If that does not describe you, you should have no trouble finding someone online who can lay out your handout for a modest investment.

There you have it: nine pitfalls, along with tips for avoiding them. If you follow the tips provided in these past three chapters, your presentations will likely stand out from the crowd (and in a good way). To make it easier still, read on to Chapter 5 for a step-by-step process for putting it all together.

CHAPTER 5

A Road Map Out of the Pit

"Start with doing what's necessary; then do what's possible;
and suddenly you are doing the impossible."

FRANCIS OF ASSISI

You've learned the nine pitfalls, along with some tips for avoiding each one. This chapter will help you pull it all together. If you follow this seven-step process, you can steer clear of those problems that lead to disengagement and boredom.

Step 1: Plan

I don't know who said it first, but you have no doubt heard the aphorism "Prior planning prevents poor performance." That is certainly true of planning a presentation. Planning (or lack thereof) was the theme of Chapter 2. You will recall the importance placed on having a specific purpose statement and an understanding of what your audience needs from you—as well as the importance of planning. (And starting with your purpose and content, *not* with your visual aids.) Drawing these principles together gives us a set of sub-steps in support of Step 1.

1a. Identify your audience.

To whom will you give this presentation? The more clearly and specifically you can answer this question, the more likely you are to make a connection with them and meet their needs. Remember, giving a presentation cannot be about *your* need to present; it must be about identifying and meeting your *audience's* needs. Who are these people? What is their background knowledge about your topic? What is bringing them to the occasion on which you are going to speak? How do they stand to benefit from the information you plan to give them? What decisions will they make based on your presentation?

1b. Identify your specific purpose.

Once you know who your audience is, then ask the specific purpose question: *What do you want them to think, do, or feel differently after they hear you speak?* The more clearly and specifically you can answer this question, the more successful your presentation will be. Furthermore, if your answer relates not just to one of those verbs but to two or even all three of them, the audience's experience will be that much richer. This is not as difficult as you might think! For example, if you want them to act, then you also want them to feel confident that it is the right action to take.

Once you have your specific purpose, write it down and keep it in front of you throughout the preparation process. For every bit of content you consider including, you must ask, "Does this support my specific purpose?" If it does not, then you must leave it out—no matter how appealing you think it may be. Save it for another talk with another purpose, perhaps to a different audience.

1c. Anticipate what your audience will be thinking when you start.

The most obvious question on your listeners' minds is always "What's in it for me?" Equally important is this compound question: "Who is this person and why should I listen to him/her?" These questions are so important, in fact, that they need to be answered before you even get to the podium, if possible. They should be answered by the person who is introducing you. However, the step of writing your introduction (which is *not* the same as a bio) comes much later, after you have created the rest of your content, so we will return to that in another section of the chapter.

At this stage, therefore, keep those questions in the background. Focus instead on questions related specifically to your content and purpose. Perhaps your audience will be wondering:

- Why is this person's solution the best one

to meet our needs?

- What is it about this research that is important to me?
- How does this new information connect to what I already know?

When you put yourself in your audience members' shoes and anticipate their thoughts in this way, especially this early in the preparation process, you are more likely to connect with them.

One way to anticipate what your audience is thinking about your topic is simply to *ask them*. Experienced speakers know the value of doing their audience research. When I have a speaking engagement, I will usually ask the meeting planner for names and contact info of several people likely to be in attendance, along with permission to contact them. Then I will call them—I prefer to get them on the phone, if possible, rather than email them—and ask them a few questions. What problem can my new information solve for them? What keeps them awake at night? Why do they plan to attend the meeting? What do they hope to get out of it? Remember, that huge training project I led was successful only after I asked someone what was on his mind and heard the answer "I'm afraid of getting yelled at or fired!" Know what is on their minds if you want to earn and keep their attention.

Step 2: Assemble the evidence

Once you know your specific purpose and the questions on your listeners' minds, you are ready to start gathering the material in support of your purpose. If, as is sometimes the case, you have already written a paper about your work, you may feel you have already performed this step—and in fact you may have done a substantial part of it. But remember that a paper and a presentation are different in many ways.

For one thing, a paper is usually more complete and detailed. A scientific paper, for example, will contain details of your procedures and materials that you will likely gloss over in your presentation, in favor of sharing the results and their significance. In this case, part of your specific purpose may well be to get your audience to read your paper.

Likewise, a detailed engineering report will certainly contain a great deal more information than the highlights you present live.

Therefore, you must be selective in gathering your material. What do you want to accomplish in *this presentation*, and what material will best support that purpose? What are the main points you will make from the lectern in support of your specific purpose? What examples or evidence will you provide to support of each those main points?

And perhaps most important, how do you plan to *anchor* each of those main points in your listeners' minds? The concept of an anchor is new to our discussion, and yet it is extremely important. One of my speaking mentors, Craig Valentine, was the 1999 World Champion of Public Speaking. Craig likes to say "What's loose is lost." In other words, if a concept is not anchored in your listeners' minds, they will not easily recall it later. Having an anchor for each of your main points is a key to having a memorable structure to your speech, which you will recall is important from our discussion in Chapter 3.

What is an anchor? You can think of it as a "hook" on which to hang your idea. Commonly used anchors include acronyms (e.g., "SMART" goals: Specific, Measurable, Achievable, Realistic, Time-bound), repeated letters ("Three P's of engineering success are Planning, Professionalism, and Precision"), and analogies (Did you realize the "desktop" on your computer is an analogy to a physical object?). Perhaps the most commonly used anchor by most non-technical presenters is *the story*, which I discussed in Chapter 3.

I am a strong advocate for wider use of stories in technical presentations as well, for the simple reason that they make your points memorable.

If you will refer to Chapter 3, you will recall that I gave you several questions you can use to identify the story in your work. You also picked up the A-B-C Model, which you can use to create a story containing tension—someone wants something, which they are initially prevented from attaining because of an obstacle which must be overcome. Simply put, *tension sustains attention*. When you get that oxytocin flowing in your listeners' brains, they will be more attuned to what you are telling them. They will want your solution even before they know what it consists of.

Therefore, as you are assembling the chunks of content that will support your specific purpose, be sure to consider two related questions:

1. What is the overall story of your effort to discover the solution or finding you came

up with? In other words, what did you want and what limitation of existing knowledge did you have to overcome to attain it?

2. What smaller stories or anecdotes can you weave into your supporting points to make them more memorable?

For more on how to craft stories so that they are memorable yet concise, refer to my book previously cited, *The Speaker's Quick Guide to Telling Better Stories*, especially Chapters 3 and 4.

Step 3: Write your first draft

Now that you have assembled the building blocks, it is time to start seeing how they all fit together. Different speakers use different processes for organizing and assembling their content. Dry-erase boards and sticky notes are two of my personal favorites, though you can also use a legal pad or whatever you choose to write on.

A word about outlining is in order here, because you may be wondering why creating an outline is not given as the next step. If you work well with outlines, that's great. Consider that a sub-step in creating your first draft. I outlined this book before starting to write it.

However, the traditional method of creating an outline—using nested points and sub-points—may not be in keeping with the way you think about your work. It may be too linear and hierarchical to inspire your most creative thinking. So instead of insisting that you create an outline, what I insist that you do is to use whatever method is best for you, as long as you do this one essential thing: *Write your presentation*.

That's right—I said write it. Writing out your talk offers several advantages. It forces you to think clearly about what you want to say, it gives you a chance to fine-tune your transitions and other key spots, and, by giving you a word count, it tells you how long your talk is. Not only that, but the best speeches aren't written—they're rewritten. Editing is to a speech as polishing is to a rock; it can turn it into a gem. And you can't edit what's not written down to begin with.

However, here is where many scientists and engineers fall into a trap: They write a presentation as if they were writing a paper. For the reasons discussed previously, a paper is not a presentation. When you write a paper, chances are that you carefully avoid the use of the second person: words like *you* and *your*. But when you are talking to a live audience of real people who are in the room with you, of course it is appropriate to use those words, because they refer to those real people, not to an abstraction.

Also, a live talk is no place to show off your extensive vocabulary, nor your command of convoluted sentence structure and syntax. Here is the place to follow the ever-popular "KISS" acronym: Keep It Short and Simple. A reader of your paper may be able to go back and re-read a complex sentence. He may be able to look up a word and then return to reading. A listener has neither of those luxuries.

It takes considerable practice to be able to write in your "speaking voice." So here is a shortcut:

Find someone to talk to—over a cup of coffee, if

necessary—and talk through your presentation, recording it as you go using either your smartphone or a dedicated voice recorder. Then either transcribe the recording yourself or—better yet—pay someone a modest amount to do that for you. (Why is the latter choice better? Because it forces you to use understandable language.) There is your first draft!

Step 4: Refine and edit

Once you have a written first draft, your next step is to edit it. As you look to revise and improve your first draft, keep in mind that editing has several objectives. You may need to edit for *time, clarity,* or *flow.*

To *edit for time* means to be aware of your word count, which is most likely shown to you on your computer screen. Unless you have timed yourself to know your speaking rate, use the conservative figure of 125 words per minute. Of the total time allotted for your presentation, be sure to subtract whatever amount you want to reserve for a question-and-answer (Q&A) session. Then subtract a minute or two for someone to introduce you. Multiply the number of minutes left by 125, and that is your target length. In equation form (times are in minutes):

Total time - Q&A - intro = speaking time
Speaking time x 125 = target word count

For example, let's say you have one hour. You anticipate up to ten minutes' worth of questions. For a one-hour presentation, a two-minute introduction is not excessive.

That leaves you 48 minutes, which works out to 6,000 words. If your word count is 7,000, you have some work to do! The numbers do not lie.

$$60 - 10 - 2 = 48$$
$$48 \times 125 = 6,000$$

If your word count exceeds your time limit by a significant amount (say, more than 10%), you probably will not be able to trim it enough by simply eliminating extra words here and there. You will need to decide what chunk(s) of content must be jettisoned in the interest of time. This is where you will return to your specific purpose for guidance. What have you included in your first draft that does not clearly support that purpose? Eliminate it.

You must also *edit for clarity*. Here is where it is useful to have a "test audience" (which may be only one person) to present your talk to. Select someone who will have a similar level of background knowledge to your anticipated audience, but someone who is not already familiar with your work. Give them your presentation and ask for feedback on anything that is not clear.

Finally, *edit for flow*. This is an indication that you have created a robust structure for your talk. If you can get through it smoothly and don't have any difficulty remembering what comes next—and if your test audience can recall and repeat your main points—then you have a presentation that flows well. If not, take another look at your main points and how they are related. Does one build upon another? Are they in the most logical order? Are the relationships between them clear and signaled by your transitions? These are questions to ask as you edit for flow.

Step 5: Create your visuals

Notice how late in the process this step comes! Were you desperate for a way to illustrate one or more of your points as you presented your first draft to a test audience? Good! That desire points to where you most need visuals. And it may not be where you first thought.

Now you are ready to avoid those pitfalls detailed in Chapter 4. Remember, your slides are merely visual aids. They are not the presentation; you are. Now that you know what you want to say, what images or visual evidence is required to help you say it and fulfill your specific purpose?

Avoid the trap of thinking that every visual in your technical *paper* needs to be included in your technical *talk*. Remember, part of your purpose may be to get your audience to read that paper, so there is no need to cram all of it into your presentation.

Also remember what was said in the last chapter about resolution and legibility. If you must put words on the screen, try using short phrases that (a) do not compete with you for your listeners' attention, (b) accentuate what you are saying, and (c) are memorable. When it is necessary to use information graphics such as charts, graphs, table, or diagrams, do not make the mistake of simply lifting them from your paper or other printed matter. They may need to be edited for clarity of display.

When you do not need to have either words or images on

the screen, and you want your audience's full attention on you, insert a black slide. (In some display programs, tapping the "B" key will also make the screen go dark; however, you will then return to the slide you have just displayed. If you want to leave that and go on, it is necessary to insert a black slide.)

As you are considering what visual aids to use during your presentation, this is also the time to give thought to your handout. This is likely to be the best place to put your detailed visual evidence. Your audience will be able to consider it on their own time, and they will walk out with a physical reminder of you and your presentation. Be sure to allow time in your preparation schedule for creating this handout as well.

Step 6: Write your introduction

When I say "introduction" in this context I do not mean the opening paragraphs of your presentation. I mean the introduction you write for someone else to give before you speak. This introduction has a specific purpose: *to engage the audience's interest and curiosity so they will want to hear what you have to say.* True, the first 30 seconds of your speech will have a major impact on whether this goal is actually accomplished, but capturing that interest starts before you even take the stage.

Do not skip this step. *Write an introduction, not a bio.* The difference is simple: A bio is about the speaker; an intro is about the speech and why the audience should care about it. If you are working with a meeting planner who requests a bio, remember that is something that will go into the event program so that the planner can show off the caliber of the speakers at the event. That is not the same purpose as an introduction.

When you write your introduction, therefore, do not focus on your academic credentials, as they will probably be available elsewhere. Focus instead on two things:

1. What benefit the audience will get from hearing you talk, and
2. What qualifies you to give this talk right now.

Notice that the answer to No. 2 does not require your complete *curriculum vitae*. It requires only enough information to satisfy me, the listener, that I am hearing from someone qualified to speak on this topic. Where you received all your degrees may or may not be relevant to this question.

How long should an introduction be? Just long enough to accomplish those two purposes. To some extent, its length will reflect the length of your talk, in the sense that in a long presentation you are bargaining for more of the audience's time and therefore they are entitled to more benefits in return for that time. Even so, a one-hour or longer talk probably does not require more than a two-minute intro. For a shorter talk, even two minutes may feel excessive.

Step 7: Rehearse

It always baffles me, when one considers how much may be riding on a successful presentation, why more presenters don't take time to fully rehearse their presentations. This is an essential step.

You may have rehearsed in front of a test audience when

you were polishing and editing your first draft. That's great! If you can get in front of that same test audience again, perhaps they can give you feedback on what improvement they have seen since that stage. Or you may want a new test audience who will not be biased by what they heard before. You can make a case for either one.

In either case, the key to your success is learning to accept feedback graciously. Make note of it and don't argue with it. That doesn't mean that every well-intentioned suggestion for improvement is a good one; it just means that you will decide that in your own time. Everyone who tells you, "This is what I heard, saw, or felt" is offering you a gift. If enough people heard something that is quite different from what you intended, then you might want to consider changes. If there is only one outlying data point, on the other hand, perhaps no change is warranted.

Where do you find a willing test audience of people who know how to give helpful feedback? The best place I know of is a Toastmasters® club[5]. I am a huge advocate for Toastmasters. I could not possibly have made the transition from broadcast engineering to professional public speaking without the help and support of my Toastmasters clubs. One club I know structures its meetings specifically to give people like me the time to try out parts of major new presentations before I get in front of paying audiences. Even if that is not your objective, I encourage you to find a local club in which you can practice and learn to give and receive feedback. This

[5] www.toastmasters.org

does not come naturally to most people. It is an acquired skill. And it is one that you need to acquire if you are going to be a successful communicator.

When you do rehearse, I also encourage you to capture your rehearsals on video. This is the most sure-fire way of seeing how you can improve. Several years ago, I learned a four-step process for using such videos methodically to improve my speaking, and I share that process in the Appendix.

There you have it: seven steps that, if followed, will lead you away from the pitfalls that reduce engagement and lead to a bored, disconnected audience. If you follow this process, then you will be far better prepared than the bulk of the technical presenters I have seen.

There is one other thing you need to prepare for, though, and that is the unscripted portion of your presentation: the dreaded Q&A. That is the topic of the next chapter.

CHAPTER 6

Prepare for the Unscripted Q&A

"I don't pretend we have all the answers. But the questions
are certainly worth thinking about."

ARTHUR C. CLARKE

Congratulations! You've put your presentation together
and rehearsed it, and you are ready to go. But there
is one more step in your preparation, and it's the
part you may never feel fully prepared for. It's the dreaded
question-and-answer (Q&A) session, where many a train of
thought has derailed. The very nature of Q&A implies some
lessening of control on the part of the speaker, and that can
be scary. The good news is that a well-handled Q&A can
enhance the audience's perception of you as an expert. If you
keep these five tips in mind, you're much more likely to keep

your audience engaged and impress them with your poise and expertise.

Universal Q&A tips

1. Never ask, "Are there any questions?" This question puts your listeners on the spot, especially if it comes at the end of the presentation. Instead, always assume there are questions, and elicit them thusly: "This would be a good spot for me to pause and take some of your questions. Who has the first short, specific question to get us started?"

2. When you've asked for questions, stop talking! Don't restate anything or add a thought you suddenly remembered. Create silence and make it clear by your body language and probing eye contact that that silence will be filled only by someone in the audience asking a question. Count silently to yourself, "One, one thousand, two, one thousand..." and be prepared to wait for ten seconds for someone to speak up. Ten seconds sounds like nothing, but it is an uncomfortably long time—someone is bound to speak up before then. (Watch and count next time you see a speaker ask for questions; hardly anyone waits for more than two or three seconds for a response.)

3. Ask your own question if necessary. In the unlikely event that no one has spoken up after you've waited ten seconds— or if you just can't wait that long (it takes practice!)—you must then defuse the tension by asking a question yourself, using this technique: say, "A question I am often asked at this point is..." and proceed to ask and answer your own question. Make it real and make it relevant. You'll need to have this question in mind before you start. This technique is preferable to "planting" a question with an audience member. Once you've asked and answered your own question, ask, "Now who has the next one?" and you should be able to get the ball rolling.

4. Repeat the question. Regardless of the audience size or the room acoustics, it is best to develop the habit of always repeating (or, if necessary, restating) a question before you answer it. If the room is large, this is essential— especially if you are using a microphone. If you don't repeat the question, you are excluding those who didn't hear it clearly from the discussion at the very time that you are supposed to be engaging them. Even if acoustics aren't the issue, there are three other reasons you should always repeat the question: (1) Doing so honors the person who asked it by demonstrating active listening. (2) Restating ensures that you have understood the question accurately. (3) The few seconds it takes to restate a question will help you in formulating your best answer.

5. Never finish with Q&A. I know this sound counterintuitive because practically every technical presentation you have ever attended has ended with Q&A. That doesn't make it right! Why do you want to do something different than what you see most presenters so? Because for you to accomplish your specific purpose, you must be memorable. That means being memorable right up to the end. And what is more forgettable than a presenter finishing with, "Well…if there are no more questions…then, I guess…thank you very much"?

Here is what you do instead. When you near the end of your presentation, say this: "I have a couple of minutes of closing remarks. Before I get to those, I know you must have questions and we have a few minutes to address those now. Who has the first short, specific question to get us started?" Notice I said "closing remarks" and not "conclusion." This is because the word "conclusion" has a specific meaning in a scientific paper or presentation, and you will have stated your conclusion before now.

When you have used up your allotted Q&A time, then you say, "That's all the questions we have time for right now. You can also submit your questions by email" (because your email address will be on the screen at this point). "And now here are the closing remarks that I promised you..." This is where you launch into the final minute or two of your *prepared* presentation. You don't introduce new information at this point, because then people will not have the chance to ask questions about it.

Instead, you want to sum up your presentation in a memorable way. You might use a story or other illustration that ties together a common thread running through your points. (For example, I have closed a one-hour presentation to scientists on the topic of presentation skills by using the Galileo story you read in Chapter 3. It takes less than two minutes.) You might circle back to the opening by saying, "I promised you would pick up three new methods for doing X and as you have seen, those methods are...A, B, C." In the case of scientific research, you might point out a promising area for future research that will build upon your findings. The point is, you leave them with something memorable. Not, "Well, I guess that's all the questions."

One final note about doing this: Because it is so "against the grain" so to speak, be sure to let your meeting planner or moderator know what you are doing ahead of time, so that he or she does not come up and try to usher you off the stage prematurely.

If you follow the five tips just given, you will be better prepared than most presenters to handle the free-form Q&A session. However, not every situation you may encounter is covered above. In the course of giving your presentations, you may encounter one of the following situations.

The show-off

Sometimes, the person who rises to ask a question is not really looking for additional information. Instead, they may simply be trying to highjack your audience and show off what they know. This is usually revealed in the form of a long-winded prologue, which may or may not be followed by an actual question.

When this happens, try not to let it get the best of you. Your audience is probably smart enough to understand what is happening, and they will likely show their impatience or displeasure—so there is no need for you to do so.

What you can do is to try to head this off by the way you ask for questions. Notice that I have twice repeated the phrase, "short, specific question." If you have already done this, you have laid the groundwork. Now you have earned the right to interrupt the long-winded questioner by saying, "And your short, specific question is…?" If your audience chuckles at this, so much the better—you need not embarrass your questioner into silence if the audience does it for you!

The hostile questioner

Perhaps you are presenting information on a controversial topic. Or perhaps your scientific findings call others' findings into question. It is not hard to imagine a situation where someone in the audience may be hostile to your point of view.

When that happens, your audience may become uncomfortable, simply because conflict makes most people uncomfortable. To accomplish your task of putting the audience's needs first, therefore, you need to acknowledge the situation and try to gently defuse it without becoming hostile or argumentative.

Start with your restatement. "So your question is, how could we have reached such a different conclusion than so many capable researchers who have gone before us?" Notice that we are slipping in a sly compliment to those, like your questioner, who may hold a different view. Never say anything that might be taken as a put-down, or the hostility is likely to spread.

Then go to a point of agreement. "Well, I'm sure we can agree that we have to go where the data lead us, and as we have seen…" and then restate how your data lead to your conclusion.

Acknowledge that you never have the final answer, as any scientist would likely agree. Then ask your questioner if you have addressed his or her question—even if you must agree to disagree. That is ultimately more satisfying than leaving the impression that you have dodged the question.

If you will maintain your composure and treat even a hostile questioner as someone who simply wants more information—even if by their demeanor they seem to want to start an argument—you will gain respect in the eyes of your audience members.

As you have seen, the unscripted Q&A session need not be a stumbling block in your effort to make (and maintain) a connection with your audience. The reason you rarely see Q&A done this way is so many technical presenters are thinking only about *their* opportunity to present *their* information. They are not thinking about being audience-focused and creating engagement. When you focus on the needs of your audience, you will realize that they deserve to have their questions addressed and handled in a way that is on par with the excellence of your entire presentation. Follow the tips in this chapter, and you will be doing exactly that.

EPILOGUE

The Result You Can Expect: Connection!

"Perhaps the most important thing we ever give
each other is our attention."

RACHEL NAOMI REMEN

Ask most technical presenters what they are trying to accomplish, and they are likely to say, "To get my information across." But as you have now seen, there are many impediments to doing just that. Give a presentation with no structure and no stories, and it is likely to be quickly forgotten. Fail to take your audience's needs into account, and your audience will not be well served by your content. Focus exclusively on narrating your slides, and you will not keep anyone's attention.

There is an alternative to these dreary outcomes. That alternative consists of a technical presentation that is engaging, understandable, and memorable, given by a presenter who displays confidence and skill. You can be that presenter. All that is required is to let go of some of the conventional wisdom about what a presentation is, and how to prepare and deliver it. And to replace that conventional wisdom with the insights and tips in this book.

Clearly, that means going against the grain in some respects. And I would not ask you any more than I would ask my coaching clients to do so, if it were not for the benefit that you and your audience stand to gain from your doing so. What is that benefit?

In a word: connection. When you connect with your audience and give them a way to connect with you, then they will connect with your content in an entirely new way. When you use stories to create empathy, for example, you will actually change your listeners' brain chemistry (legally, and temporarily) in a way that makes them more receptive to what you have to say. In short...

Connection before Content; Empathy before Evidence

Had I known that in Texas in the early 1990s, I could have saved myself a lot of time and grief. But I know that now—and so do you.

APPENDIX

Watching Yourself on Video

You've rehearsed your presentation and captured it on video, as recommended in Chapter 5. Now what?

What you do next depends on the strength of your desire to improve. For my purposes, I'm going to assume you're not one of those speakers who will simply let that video languish, un-viewed. Instead, you want to use your video as a learning tool. How do you do that? By reviewing it, obviously. But some strategies for doing so are more effective than others. Here is a four-step process you can use that I believe will give you the best results.

Step 1: Watch the video with the sound turned off. That's right—don't listen to it! On this first pass, start to develop the habit of asking questions about *the speaker* in third person. This will help you begin to be more objective than we can typically be when watching ourselves on video. (Not hearing your own voice will help with this.) Don't ask "What do *I* look like?" or "What the heck was *I* doing?" Instead, ask questions like, "How well does the speaker use the stage? What is the speaker's body language saying here? How well does the speaker seem to be engaged with the audience? Where is that engagement the strongest or the weakest?"

Step 2: Turn your back to the screen (or turn your video monitor off) and just listen. This is the opposite of Step 1. Now you want sound and no visual. Again, ask your questions in the third person: Does the speaker have a coherent message? Does she deliver it without repeating herself or stumbling over transitions? Are the stories engaging and clearly related to his points? Is his intention clear? Do I understand what the speaker wants the listeners to think, do, or feel differently by the end?

Step 3: Watch the video again, but at faster-than-normal playback speed. This is not hard to do with most video programs (or, if you're old-school, a DVD player). Chances are, you won't have audio, and that's fine. This time you are watching for repeated physical mannerisms that will become evident when you speed up the video. What does the speaker do with his hands? Does she push her hair back frequently? If you think you're watching a tennis match, perhaps the speaker paces back and forth excessively. These are the kinds of things that come out when you watch it sped up.

Step 4: Watch and listen normally. Be sure to save this step for last. Now that you have practiced some third-person objectivity in your viewing, apply that here. How well does the speaker get and hold your attention? How would you rate the speaker's overall effectiveness? Are the voice, body, and face congruent with the words being spoken? Does the speaker come across as someone the audience can relate to? What would you advise the speaker to do differently next time?

Once you have made it through all four of these passes, congratulations! You have taken a big step toward improving your next presentation.

ABOUT THE AUTHOR

Since 2011, speaker, coach, trainer, and author David P. Otey has helped thousands of people on two continents in their quest for personal and professional growth. Before that, he worked in television engineering, holding the highest level of professional certification from the Society of Broadcast Engineers. He received a BA in Radio-Television-Film and Physics from Trinity University and both an MA in Communication and an MBA from the University of Texas. David is the author of *The Speaker's Quick Guide to Telling Better Stories* (2017) as well as a contributing author to the book *World Class Speaking in Action* (2015), the *NAB Engineering Handbook, Tenth Edition* (2007), and various periodicals. A native of Port Arthur, Texas, he currently resides in Golden, Colorado.

Contact David by email at david@davidotey.com. Follow him on twitter @AuthorDavidOtey or at Facebook/OteySpeaking.

Made in the USA
Lexington, KY
27 September 2019